HOT WHEELS

*AN INNER RING HIPSTER*
Michael Hardcastle
Illustrated by Ron Sandford

Ernest Benn London & Tonbridge

# 1

'Lie down on the path,' said Lindy.
'I'm going to jump over you.'
Tommy looked at her in amazement.
He thought she was joking.
But Lindy, hands on hips,
wasn't smiling.
She had a very determined look
on her face.

'Go on, Tommy.
I won't hurt you, I promise.
If this trick works, I'll let you have
my old crash gloves.'

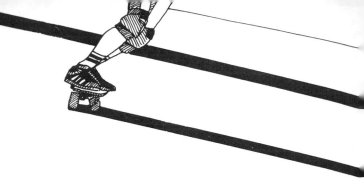

'Give them to me, you mean?'
Tommy wanted to be sure.

'Well, O.K. –
but you've got to let me practise
this trick until I get it
dead right.'
'If you land on me
I'll be dead all right,'
Tommy muttered.
But he was keen to have the gloves.

He and Lindy were
about the same size
so he knew they would fit him.
Both were very slim
but while Lindy had hair
the colour of carrots,
Tommy was fair-haired.

'Why can't you just jump over
a log or a box?' Tommy asked.
'Because jumping over a person
makes it real. It makes you try
really hard.'

Unhappily, he lay flat on the path.
He was face down
because he didn't want to see
how close she would be to landing
on him.

7

Lindy hurried up the slope,
carrying her red and black board.
She was sure she could do the trick
because she'd practised it often.
It worked nine times out of ten.
But she wasn't going to tell Tommy
she missed out on it sometimes!

Down the slope she came,
building up speed all the way.
Her crouch was low and
she was perfectly balanced.
Tommy was playing his part well.
He didn't even lift his head
to see how near she was.
Then, just as she seemed
about to run into him,
Lindy flicked the skateboard
to one side —
and leaped into the air.

She jumped right over Tommy
and landed so easily that
she didn't stumble at all.
'Hey, great!' she yelled.
'Told you it would work.'
Tommy hurriedly got to his feet,
before she could try the trick again.

'Let's go and get the gloves,'
he said eagerly.
He wasn't going to let her
change her mind. Lindy nodded,
and they set off across the park.

Many times he had fallen
and scraped his hands because
he hadn't any real
skateboarder's gloves.
Now his hands would be safe
from cuts and scratches.

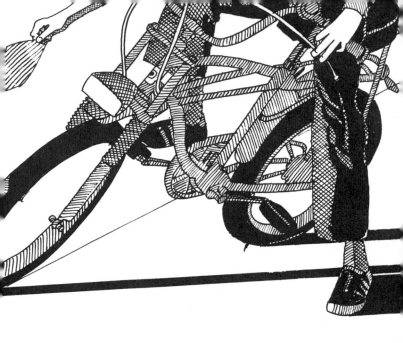

# 2

Just as they reached Lindy's home
they saw Alan coming down the road
on his bike. As usual,
he seemed to be in a hurry.
When he spotted them
he waved a piece of paper.
'Heard about the circus?' he asked,
jumping off his bike.
Together, they shook their heads.

Lindy was surprised that
Alan was interested in a circus.
Alan spent nearly all
his free time making money,
by swapping and selling anything
he could get his hands on.

'It's coming here next week,'
Alan told them. 'Great thing is
that they're running a skateboard
contest as part of the show.
Calling it 'Hot Wheels'
– a free-style contest
for the best trick on a skateboard.'

'Hey, great!' Lindy exclaimed.
'Can anyone have a go?'

'Sure, and there are some big prizes.
The Hot Wheels contest is on
the last night of the show.
The Big Top will be packed out.'

Lindy knew what Alan was thinking.
If he won the contest
a lot of people would know about him,
and so he'd get more customers.
But she thought Alan was too heavy
to be good at free-style
skateboarding. His weight was O.K.
for speed skating or slalom;
but not for anything else.

Tommy was thinking about
the sort of trick he could try.
He wanted to do something
that would surprise them all.
So he would have to work on it
– by himself. Those gloves
would be very useful now.

'Lindy,' he said. 'I think
you've got something of mine. . . . '

'O.K. See you,' said Alan
and rode off at speed.
It wasn't long before he came
to a small shop. The window was
piled high with all kinds of junk;
clothes, books, old machines
and boxes.

14

Alan walked in.
He was well known there
and the man in the shop
smiled at him.
'What is it today?' he asked.
'Are you buying or selling?'
'Buying,' Alan replied.
'I want some grip-tape
for skateboards. Plenty of it.'
'No problem,' the man told him,
and he lifted a couple of boxes
off a shelf.

Alan liked the green tape best,
and he said he'd take the lot.
Some of it he would use
on his own skateboard and he knew
he would have plenty of customers
for the rest.

For free-style riding,
a good gripping surface
on the deck of the board
was very important.

As soon as he got home
Alan went to the shed in the garden
where he worked on his gear.
He scrubbed hard at the wooden deck
of his skateboard to get it
perfectly clean.
Then he took out the bolts
that joined the trucks to the deck.
Next, he fixed the grip-tape
to the deck in long strips.

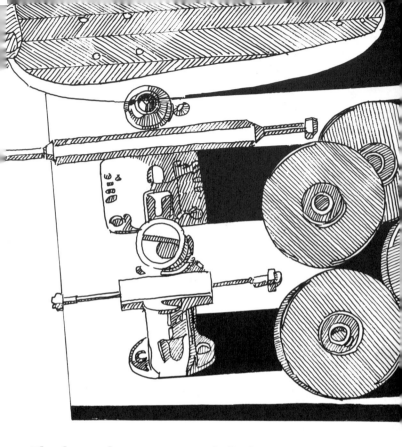

The last job was to punch holes
in the tape where the bolts
were placed. If the tape had been put
over the bolt-heads it wouldn't have
gripped properly. It would have
come loose from the metal.
He put the bolts back
and the board was ready for use.

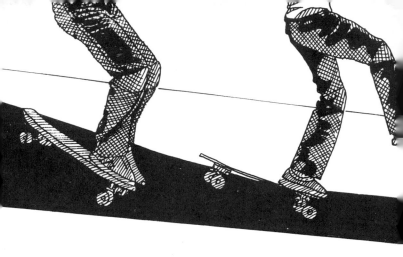

Now he had to test it.
It was too late to go far
but he could go to the church.
A steep path ran
through the churchyard.
Many people used it as a short cut
but skateboarding was banned.

Alan decided to take a chance.
He knew he would have to practise
some new tricks to have a chance
of winning the contest.
He was good at speed skating
and slalom because he could use
the power in his legs. But power
wouldn't be much use in free-style.

# 3

On his way to the church
he tried to work out some new ideas.
There was no one about
when he arrived at the church.
It was already getting dark.

As he went along the path
the head-stones on the graves
seemed like silent watchers.
He tried to ignore them.
As soon as he got on his board
he felt better:
he could ignore everything
except skateboarding.

The grip-tape made control easier
as he tried a few kick-turns.
Alan moved on to doing wheelies
– putting both feet together
over the front wheels,
then pressing down
to lift the tail of the board.
Without grip-tape,
he could never have done
a nose wheelie because his feet
would have slipped off the deck.
But even so, he managed only one
really good wheelie.

But Alan didn't give up easily.
Then, just as he was getting better,
he heard a noise behind him.
His heart almost stopped.

Next moment a huge dog dashed out
from behind a head-stone.
It leaped straight at Alan.

'Down, Rollo!' a man called.
He had been walking his dog
through the churchyard.
Rollo took no notice.
The dog hated skateboarders
and when he saw one he attacked.

21

'That dog's out of control,'
Alan shouted angrily,
trying to keep the dog off.
'It'll kill someone one day.'

'Probably a skateboarder,'
replied Rollo's owner.
'You shouldn't be in here.
Next time Rollo sees you,
you'll need two skateboards
to get away from him.
From what I can see,
you need two, anyway,
because you're so fat!'

Alan decided it was time to go.
It hadn't been a very good work-out.
But, as he reached home,
he remembered something
the dog owner had said.
Suddenly, it gave him an idea. . . .

Lindy was dancing.
She was a brilliant dancer
and a member of a display team.
Tonight the team were performing
at a supper club in the town centre.
People were sitting at tables
in a ring round the dance floor.
They clapped and clapped
when the team finished.

'Can you go back
and do something else?'
asked the man running the club.
'Something different – anything.
They don't want you to finish
just yet.'
All the girls were tired
and only Lindy was willing to have a go.
'I could do a skateboard act,'
she said. 'Just a bit of free-style,
if you like.'
'Fine,' the man told her.
'That's different, all right.'

Lindy had been practising
some new tricks and this
was the chance to try them out
in public. If the act
went down well then she could use it
for the circus contest.

The dance floor was made of
very hard wood, so it was okay
for skateboarding.
She started with
a few nose and tail wheelies,
followed by round-the-world spins.
The crowd had fallen in love
with the slim, red-haired dancer
and cheered every trick.

This made Lindy feel very confident.
So she decided to try
the hardest trick of all.
At least, it looked hard to do
but really it was fairly easy.
When it worked,
it looked very good.

Lindy moved into the centre
of the floor.
She gripped her board
with both hands,
one at the nose,
the other at the tail.

Then she ran a few steps,
put the skateboard down –
and swung herself up
into a hand-stand. When she
felt herself losing her balance,
she moved the board round
the way she was falling.
That way she kept her balance,
her legs high in the air.

'That's terrific!' yelled a man
at a table near the front.
He stood up to lead more clapping.

Lindy lowered herself to the ground
and then took a bow,
smiling happily.
With a few more tricks,
she would have a brilliant act
for the circus contest.

'That was great!' said the boss
of the club. 'We'll pay you extra
for that. It was as good as
a circus performance.'
'I hope so,' said Lindy, laughing.

A few days later
Tommy was doing his training
for the contest.

He had been riding a skateboard
a shorter time than Alan or Lindy.
But he was eager to catch up.
Tommy was always in a hurry:
he would never wait for anything.

He usually practised on a slope
under the motorway fly-over.
There he could get up a good speed
– and he was getting better
all the time at speed skating.

So far, he hadn't tried
much free-style riding.
But watching some of Lindy's tricks
had given him an idea.
Tommy was going to jump
from a moving skateboard
over a box and onto another board
– and keep moving.
He hadn't tried it out yet.
But he felt sure it would work.

He strapped on his knee pads
and then pulled on his gloves.
He was using a friend's board
for his run-up and he would jump
on to his own board.

Tommy placed his board in position:
in front of it, he put down
an empty box. Slowly
he pushed the other board
back to the start of his run.

At that moment, Lindy arrived.
When she saw
what Tommy was about to do
she yelled to him to wait.
But her voice was lost
in the noise of all the cars
on the motorway.

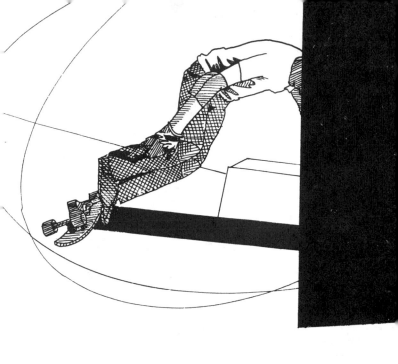

Tommy set off, building up speed,
crouching ready to jump.
His timing was good.
A split-second before the nose
of his board hit the box,
Tommy took off.

He cleared the box —
but only his heel landed
on the other skateboard,
which skidded away from him.
Tommy went up in the air,
turned over, and fell
on his shoulder. There was a crack
as the bone broke.
Tommy passed out.

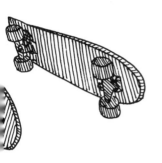

# 4

When he opened his eyes
Lindy was bending over him.
The pain was awful
and he couldn't even speak.

'Don't move, Tommy, don't move,'
Lindy told him. 'I'll get help.'

At the hospital
the doctor told Tommy
it might have been worse.
'It's a clean break
but it'll keep you out of action
for a few weeks.'

They'd given Tommy something
to take the pain away
and he felt very tired.
But all he could think about
was missing the contest.

Lindy knew he had been crazy
to try a trick like that
on his own. But she also knew
how he was feeling,
so she said nothing about it.
Tommy had gone through enough.

On the day the circus arrived,
Lindy went along to see the animals.
She took Tommy with her
to cheer him up.
Tommy had his arm in a sling.
He had been told
not to touch a skateboard again
until his shoulder mended.

'Let's see the lions first,' said Lindy.
When she reached their cage
she stared at them for a long time.
'I just hope they don't get out
when I'm performing,' she said.
'You'd have to save me, Tommy.'
It was the wrong thing to say.
With only one arm he could use,
Tommy was helpless.
She hurried him away
to see the monkeys –
and at least they made him laugh.
The men were putting up the Big Top.
As Lindy and Tommy watched them,
Alan arrived. He'd come to see
what kind of skating bowl
would be used for the contest.

'I check up on everything,'
he added. 'I leave nothing to chance.'
Lindy nodded.
'I know,' she said.
She guessed that Alan was hoping
to have a practice run as well.
But he was out of luck.
The skate bowl wasn't to be used
until the night of the contest.

The Big Top was full —
of people, of noise, of colour.
The circus was a sell-out.
The skate bowl had been placed
in the centre of the ring
and now the ringmaster
was introducing the performers.

Lindy was among the last to go.
Alan was just ahead of her.
One of the first riders to perform
walked the board,
changing his position on the deck
as he rode round the bowl.
The tricks he did looked good
and the crowd clapped. But
the next performer did even better:
her round-the-world spins
and kick turns were done
at great speed.

'Good luck,' Lindy said to Alan
when he was called into the ring.
To her surprise,
he was carrying two skateboards.
Alan looked more confident
than he felt: he wished
he had been able to practise
in the circus bowl.

But everything went well
until he tried to ride
the two boards together,
one on top of the other:
a double-decker.
The surface was too fast
for that trick and he fell off.

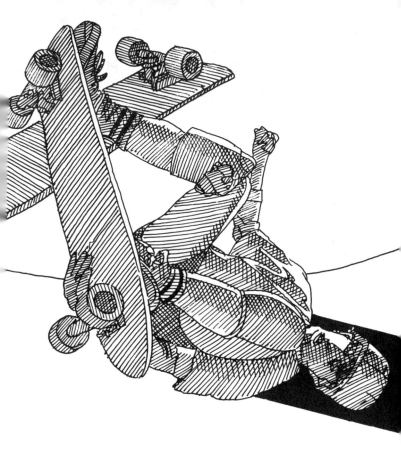

He tried again
but the same thing happened.
The crowd gave him a clap
as he left the ring
but Alan knew he had no chance
of winning.

'And now, it's the turn of
Miss Lindy Miller,'
the ringmaster called.

Lindy was used to performing
in front of a lot of people,
so she wasn't nervous.
Her riding was smooth
and she did some very fast spins
without a mistake.
Her skills and balance as a dancer
helped her to perform
with plenty of style.

The crowd clapped loudly
when she went into a hand-stand.

That gave her extra confidence
for her best trick,
the one she had been practising
ever since she had heard
about the contest.

Lindy lowered her feet
back onto the board
and picked up speed again
for another hand-stand.
But this time she bent her elbows
until she was resting
on her fore-arms.
She kept one leg high in the air.

Slowly, she bent her other leg
until her foot was just touching
the top of her head.

Very cleverly,
she held that position
as her board rolled easily
round the skate bowl.
Some people in the crowd
stood up to clap and cheer.

Lindy was pretty and her red hair
made her stand out.
But it was her skills and style
that made her a winner.

Soon the ringmaster was calling
her name again. 'Miss Lindy Miller,
the clear winner of the Hot Wheels
Contest.'

Lindy jumped high in the air
with happiness – and then ran back
into the centre of the ring
to collect her prize
and take a bow.

RED CIRCLE HIPSTERS

HOT WHEELS – Freestyle skateboarding
SNAKE RUN – Slalom skateboarding
RACING BIKE – Motocross
GO FOR GOAL – Football
by *Michael Hardcastle*

Four adventure stories about popular sports
– with tips to improve your skill.
Will Steve's loyalty to Vale stop him
signing for a top club?
Gary is going to be the best – could he prove it
by winning the Trent Park Motocross?


THE BIKE
OUT OF THE DARK
by *Barbara Ireson*

THE FORBIDDEN ROOM
THE OPEN GRAVE
by *Josephine Poole*

Four spine-chilling tales of horror and suspense.
Who is the strange boy on the bike? Why does he
know so much about Steve? Bella's husband is rich
and powerful; but why does she feel so afraid
of him? And what is the terrifyingly evil presence
in the next room of the old cottage?

RED CIRCLE HIPSTERS

DIGGING FOR TREASURE
THE SUNDAY PAPERS
FLOOD
SAUSAGES ON THE SHORE
by *Richard Parker*

Four stories about Stringer, Dave, Linda and Mag,
who live in a southern riverport town. There is the
strange 'treasure' on the river bank, the flood
rescue that never was and the new paper round
that turns out more awkward than anyone expects.

HUSH-A-BYE BABY
BLOW UP
GATE CRASHERS
NO LADDER FOR TOM BATES
by *Delia Huddy*

Carol, Nick, Val and Glenn live in a New Town.
You can read about the danger at the local
chemical factory, how they find a wounded horse
and what happens when they lose next door's baby.

GREEN CIRCLE HIPSTERS

HIGH JACKS, LOW JACKS
FIRST DAY OUT
THE ACCIDENT
THE SECRET
by *Clive King*

Four stories about Rima, a young Asian girl and
her brother Sami, who are starting a new life in
England.

FIRE ON THE SEA
CRASH CAR
HOLIDAY HOUSE
STRONG ARM
by *Michael Hardcastle*

Steve and Anna live in Rockport, a seaside town.
Read about their friends and what they do;
how they find a new sport — stock car racing,
and what happens when there is a fire on the pier.